MANASSAS
(Bull Run)

NATIONAL BATTLEFIELD PARK
Virginia

by Francis F. Wilshin

NATIONAL PARK SERVICE HISTORICAL HANDBOOK SERIES NO. 15

Washington, D.C., 1953 (Reprint 1961)

The National Park System, of which Manassas National Battlefield Park is a unit, is dedicated to conserving the scenic, scientific, and historic heritage of the United States for the benefit and inspiration of its people

MANASSAS (BULL RUN)

By Francis F. Wilshin

Trade Paperback ISBN: 1-58218-777-0

All rights reserved, which includes the right to reproduce this book or portions thereof in any form whatsoever except as provided by the U. S. Copyright Law. For information address Digital Scanning, Inc.

Digital Scanning and Publishing is a leader in the electronic republication of historical books and documents. We publish many of our titles as eBooks, as well as traditional hardcover and trade paper editions. DSI is committed to bringing many traditional and little known books back to life, retaining the look and feel of the original work.

©2004 DSI Digital Reproduction
First DSI Printing December 2004

Published by DIGITAL SCANNING, INC.
Scituate, MA 02066
Toll free: 888-349-4443
Outside U.S.: 781-545-2100

www.digitalscanning.com

Contents

THE FIRST DAYS OF THE WAR	1
CONFEDERATES LOOK TO MANASSAS DEFENSES	3
THE FEDERAL ARMY MOVES TOWARD MANASSAS	5
McDOWELL TESTS THE CONFEDERATE RIGHT	7
FIRST BATTLE OF MANASSAS	8
Morning Phase—The Fight at Matthews Hill	11
Afternoon Phase	13
Effects of First Manassas	17
WINTER'S LULL	18
PRELIMINARY OPERATIONS TO SECOND MANASSAS	19
POPE CONCENTRATES BEHIND THE RAPIDAN	20
LEE'S OPERATIONS ALONG THE RAPIDAN AND RAPPAHANNOCK	21
SECOND BATTLE OF MANASSAS	26
First Phase—Bristoe and Manassas, August 27	26
Second Phase—Groveton, August 28	27
Third Phase—Main Battle, August 29-30	27
Fourth Phase—Chantilly, September 1	36
Results of Second Battle of Manassas	37
THE WAR AFTER SECOND MANASSAS	38
GUIDE TO THE AREA	39
THE PARK	46
HOW TO REACH THE PARK	47
ADMINISTRATION	47
RELATED AREAS	47
ABOUT YOUR VISIT	47

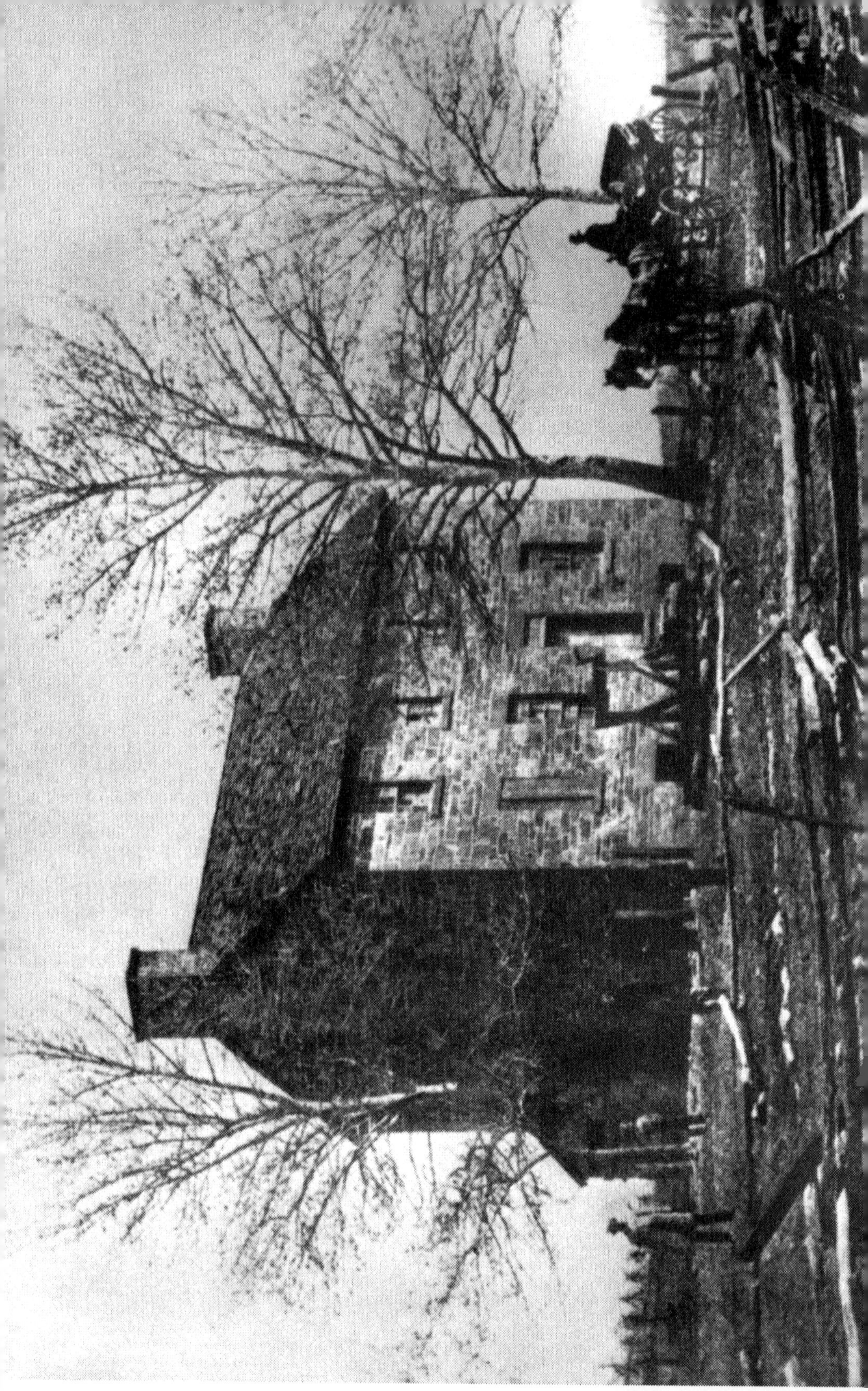

M ANASSAS NATIONAL BATTLEFIELD PARK *preserves the scene of two of the famous battles of the Civil War. The first shall be ever memorable as the opening engagement of that great conflict, while the second, fought approximately a year later, paved the way for Lee's first invasion of the North. In each instance Confederate arms won signal success and dangerously threatened the National Capital.*

The Civil War was perhaps the most dramatic and significant event in the history of the United States as an independent nation. It was the climax of a half century of social, political, and economic rivalries growing out of an economy half slave, half free. In the race for territorial expansion in the West, in the evolution of the theories of centralized government, and in the conception of the rights of the individual, these rivalries became so intense as to find a solution only in the grim realities of civil strife.

It was on the great battlefields of this war, stretching from the Mexican border to Pennsylvania, that these differences were resolved in a new concept of national unity and an extension of freedom. In the scope of its operations, in the magnitude of its cost in human life and financial resources, the war had few, if any, parallels in the past. Its imprint upon the future was deep and lasting, its heroic sacrifice an inspiring tribute to the courage and valor of the American people.

The First Days of the War

The flash and the dull roar of a 10-inch mortar, April 12, 1861, announced to a startled countryside the firing of the opening gun of the Civil War. Two days later Fort Sumter surrendered. The reverberations

Wartime photograph of the Stone House, which still stands as the most conspicuous landmark of both the First and Second Battles of Manassas. Courtesy National Archives.

of this shot were to shake the very foundations of the Nation. Gone was the period of apathy and indecision. Events now moved with lightning-like rapidity.

On April 15, Lincoln issued his call for 75,000 volunteers, and soon troops were pouring into Washington. On May 23, Virginia voted to ratify the Ordinance of Secession, and the next day columns of Federal troops crossed the Potomac and seized Alexandria and Arlington Heights. Eight days later Richmond became the capital of the Confederacy and the chief objective of the Federal armies in the East. Stretching from the Ohio to Chesapeake Bay, Virginia constituted the wealthiest and most populous state of the Confederacy. Here were to be found rich natural resources and a heavy network of railroads and highways for military transport. These military advantages, however, were somewhat offset by the deep waters which flanked much of the state, increasing its vulnerability to Federal attack.

Straight across the path of one of the main high roads to Richmond from the north lay Manassas, a small railroad settlement, only a few miles east of the Bull Run Mountains. Here the Orange and Alexandria Railroad formed a junction with the Manassas Gap line which extended westward through the Blue Ridge to Strasburg, near Winchester. By seizure of this significant junction, located approximately 25 miles southwest of Washington, the Federal army could follow the Orange and Alexandria southwest to Gordonsville and thence proceed by the Virginia Central eastward to Richmond. This, with good supporting highways, would assure an overland approach that would avoid many of the natural barriers found in the shortest route by Aquia Creek and Fredericksburg.

The significance of Manassas was likewise apparent to the Confederates. As early as May 6, Col. St. George Cocke, commanding the Potomac Department, had received a dispatch from Gen. Robert E. Lee: "You are desired to post at Manassas Gap Junction a force sufficient to defend that point against an attack likely to be made against it by troops from Washington."

The first troops to arrive were two raw, undrilled, and ununiformed Irish regiments from Alexandria, armed with altered muskets. By May 14, Cocke was able to write Lee that he had succeeded in assembling a force of 918 men at Manassas. That he had a clear grasp of the military significance of the area is seen in his dispatch to Lee the next day: "It is obvious, sir, with a strong *corps d'armee* at Manassas, and at least a division at Winchester, these two bodies being connected by a continuous railway through Manassas Gap, there should be kept at all times upon that road ample means of transportation. These two columns—one at Manassas and one at Winchester—could readily co-operate and concentrate upon the one point or the other." Here then was a significant germ of Confederate strategy.

As a phase of this strategy, Brig. Gen. Joseph E. Johnston had been sent to take command of the Confederate force of about 12,000 men stationed in the northern end of the Shenandoah Valley at Harper's Ferry. Here was the gateway to the North through the Cumberland Valley of Maryland and here passed the great Baltimore and Ohio Railroad which connected Washington with the West. But Maj. Gen. Winfield Scott, then in command of the Army of the United States, had dispatched Maj. Gen. Robert Patterson with a force of about 18,000 men to seize this strategic position and to prevent, at all odds, the junction of Johnston's forces with the Confederate army at Manassas.

Confederates Look to Manassas Defenses

On June 1, Brig. Gen. Pierre G. T. Beauregard, the Confederate hero of Fort Sumter, arrived to take command at Manassas. Two days later he was writing President Jefferson Davis requesting reinforcements. At this early date the defenses of Manassas appeared anything but formidable to the eyes of an English lieutenant of artillery who, arriving at night, viewed them for the first time: "I could scarcely believe that this was a great military depot, there being nothing within my range of vision to indicate that such was the fact. The station itself was a low, one-storied building, about seventy-five feet in length, with bales and boxes scattered about; a house of refreshment close by was uninviting, and except one or two small cottages scattered here and there, naught was to be seen."

Brig. Gen. Pierre Gustave Toutant Beauregard in command of the Confederate Army of the Potomac. Courtesy National Archives.

By the end of June this picture had materially changed. The roads, the fields, and the town were filled with soldiers by the thousands. Around the junction massive fortifications had been erected running out in different directions from the station. Through the embrasures of these earthworks the muzzles of heavy cannon pointed menacingly toward Washington. Acres of trees had been felled to give free range to artillery, and at key positions along the front men were constantly on guard at their battle stations. Camps had sprung up like mushrooms in the open countryside, and here troops in and out of uniform could be seen almost incessantly engaged in drill.

By June 23, Beauregard was able to advise the Confederate Secretary of War that, in consequence of large reinforcements lately received, he had been able to divide his forces into six brigades commanded by Bonham, Ewell, D. R. Jones, Terrett, Cocke, and Early. Advance detachments had been stationed at key points including Centreville, Fairfax Court House, Germantown, the junction of the Old Braddock Road with the Fairfax Court House Road, and at Sangster's Crossroads. With the main body of his troops partially intrenched along Bull Run, from Union Mills to the Stone Bridge, Beauregard watched closely the Federal preparations for an advance.

As the tension mounted, alarms occurred with increasing frequency. Bootless, hatless, and coatless men often dashed to assembly sounded by the "thump, thump of the big drums." Rumors of the Federal advance "filled every breeze." In a dispatch, dated July 9, Beauregard informed President Davis: "Enemy's force increasing, and advancing daily this side of Potomac. He will soon attack with very superior numbers. No time should be lost in re-enforcing me here with at least ten thousand men—volunteers or militia."

On the 17th Beauregard telegraphed President Davis informing him of an attack on his outposts and requesting that he send reinforcements "at the earliest possible moment." Confronted with this crisis, Davis acted quickly. Advising Beauregard of the dispatch of reinforcements of Hampton's Legion, McRae's regiment, and two battalions of Mississippi and Alabama troops, he ordered Holmes' troops up from Fredericksburg. The same day, through his adjutant, he sent the following dispatch to Johnston in Winchester:

RICHMOND, *July* 17, 1861.

General J. E. JOHNSTON, *WINCHESTER, Va.*:

General Beauregard is attacked. To strike the enemy a decisive blow a junction of all your effective force will be needed. If practicable, make the movement, sending your sick and baggage to Culpeper Court-House either by railroad or by Warrenton. In all the arrangements exercise your discretion.

S. COOPER,
Adjutant and Inspector General.

Realizing that Harper's Ferry was untenable, Johnston had previously retired upon Winchester, with Patterson in cautious pursuit. Receiving Davis' dispatch at 1 a. m., July 18, Johnston determined to elude Patterson and join Beauregard as quickly as possible. By a forced march he reached Piedmont where his various brigades entrained for Manassas Junction, 35 miles away. Brig. Gen. Thomas J. Jackson's brigade was in advance, followed by those of Bee, Bartow, and Elzey.

Thus, after approximately 3 months of hurried preparation following Sumter, the stage was finally set—the drama of the opening battle was about to unfold.

The Federal Army Moves Toward Manassas

On July 16, Brig. Gen. Irvin McDowell had reluctantly put the Federal army in motion. In vain he had attempted to delay the movement until adequate training could provide him with an effective fighting force composed of the 3-year volunteers, authorized by President Lincoln on May 3, but popular clamor would not be denied. Pressure for a forward movement was heightened by the realization that the term of enlistment was rapidly expiring for a large body of the troops. Further delay would mean the loss of their services.

With excitement and high expectancy, the army, accompanied by many notables in fine carriages, took the road 35,000 strong. Seldom had the country seen such a splash of color as was presented by the brilliant

Brig. Gen. Irvin McDowell, in command of the Federal Army in the First Battle of Manassas. Courtesy National Archives.

uniforms of the various regiments and the gaily fluttering national and regimental flags. The first day's advance covered only 6 miles. Oppressive heat, dust, thirst, and the weight of heavy equipment slowed the step and caused considerable straggling.

Lagging spirits, however, caught fire with the triumphant advance of Hunter's division into Fairfax Court House. As the head of the column swung into town, Confederate units stationed there fled in such haste as to leave large quantities of forage and camp equipage behind. In an impressive show of martial splendor, the troops, four abreast with fixed bayonets, paraded through the streets to the stirring strains of the national anthem and other patriotic airs struck up by the regimental bands.

From Fairfax Court House the advance moved cautiously toward Centreville, with engineers and axmen flung forward to alert the army to "masked batteries" and to clear roadblocks of fallen timber left by the retiring Confederates. By noon of the 18th the main body of McDowell's army had assembled at Centreville and now stood poised to strike.

During the advance, little or no information had been received regarding Patterson's movements in the valley. Irked by this, Scott telegraphed Patterson as follows:

Washington, July 18, 1861.

Major-General Patterson, . . .

I have certainly been expecting you to beat the enemy. If not, to hear that you had felt him strongly, or, at least, had occupied him by threats and demonstrations. You have been at least his equal, and, I suppose, superior, in numbers. Has he not stolen a march and sent reenforcements toward Manassas Junction? A week is enough to win victories. . . .

WINFIELD SCOTT

Confederate fortifications at Manassas, Va. Wartime photograph. Courtesy National Archives.

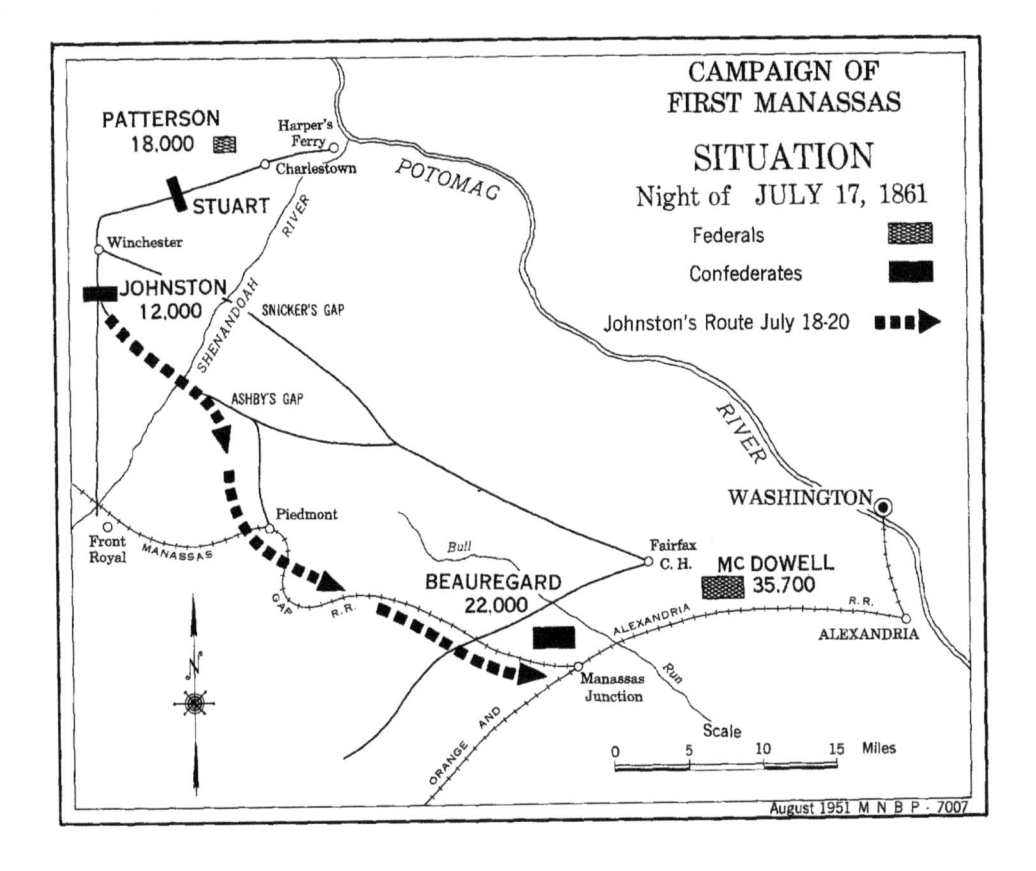

To this, Patterson sent the following reply to Colonel Townsend in Scotts' headquarters:

> CHARLESTOWN, VA., *July* 18th, 1861
>
> Col. E. D. Townsend:
>
> Telegram of to-day received. The enemy has stolen no march upon me. I have kept him actively employed, and by threats and reconnaissances in force caused him to be re-enforced. I have accomplished in this respect more than the General-in-Chief asked, or could well be expected, in face of an enemy far superior in numbers, with no line of communication to protect. . . .
>
> R. PATTERSON, . . .

The events of the next few days more than justified Scott's suspicions.

McDowell Tests the Confederate Right

On July 18, in a feeling movement on the Confederate right, Tyler made a thrust against Beauregard's troops stationed in the vicinity of Blackburn's Ford. The affair got somewhat out of hand with the result that the Federal force was smartly repulsed. The action had a depressing effect on Union morale but greatly boosted that of the Confederates. There then followed 2 days of costly delay for McDowell during which time he brought forward his supplies—a delay the Confederates were quick to capitalize upon. To the sound of the axe and the crash of falling trees, they built roadblocks along the Warrenton Pike in the vicinity of the Stone Bridge and in general strengthened their defenses. More important, the delay gave Johnston much needed time in which to reach Manassas.

Confederate reinforcements were now steadily moving in. On the 19th, Jackson arrived 2,500 strong, having covered approximately 55 miles in 25 hours. At sunrise of the 20th, more of Johnston's reinforcements had come in—the 7th and 8th Georgia regiments of Bartow's brigade numbering 1,400 men. About noon, Johnston himself arrived accompanied by Bee, the 4th Alabama, the 2d Mississippi, and two companies of the 11th Mississippi. The Confederate camp now became a scene of busy activity. While the reinforcements moved up to position in the line, Beauregard and Johnston conferred on plans for an offensive. Candles burned low in headquarters that night as Beauregard and his staff put the finishing touches to the Confederate plan of attack. At 4:30 a. m., he submitted it to Johnston, his superior, for the approval that was quickly granted. The plan involved the flanking of the Federal left, but the early movement of McDowell, the delayed arrival of expected reinforcements, and the miscarriage of orders combined to prevent its execution.

First Battle of Manassas   (SEE MAP ON PAGES 22-23.)

Sunday, July 21, dawned bright and clear. The listless stirring of the trees gave early promise that the day would be hot. Dust lay thick upon the grass, the brush, and the uniforms of the men. The Confederate camps were just beginning to stir from a restless night when, suddenly about 5:15 a. m., there was heard the thunderous roar of a big gun in the vicinity of the Stone Bridge. With this shot, fired from a 30-pounder Parrott rifle of Tyler's command, McDowell opened the first battle of the war.

Since 2:30 a. m. his troops had been in motion executing a well-conceived plan of attack. In bright moonlight, across the valley from Centreville "sparkling with the frost of steel," the Federal army had moved in a three-pronged attack. McDowell had originally planned to turn the Confederate right, but the affair of the 18th at Blackburn's Ford had shown the Confederates in considerable strength in that sector. Further informed that the Stone Bridge was mined and that the turnpike west of the bridge was blocked by a heavy abatis, he determined to turn the extreme Confederate left. By this flanking movement he hoped to

Young Confederates in Richmond who were soon to receive their baptism of fire at the First Battle of Manassas. From "Photographic History of the Civil War."

seize the Stone Bridge and destroy the Manassas Gap Railroad at or near Gainesville, thus breaking the line of communication between Johnston, supposedly at Winchester, and Beauregard at Manassas. To screen the main attack, Tyler was to make a feinting thrust at the Confederate defenses at the Stone Bridge, while Richardson was to make a diversion at Blackburn's Ford. Miles' division was to cover Centreville, while

Federal Army near Fairfax Court House en route to the First Battle of Manassas. A detachment of the 2d Ohio is shown in the foreground. From original sketch by A. R. Waud. Courtesy Library of Congress.

Runyon's division covered the road to Washington. To a large extent the success of the attack depended upon two factors—rapidity of movement and the element of surprise.

Turning to the right at Cub Run Bridge, the main Federal column, composed of Hunter's and Heintzelman's divisions, had followed a narrow dirt road to Sudley Ford which they reached, after exasperating delays, about 9:30 a. m. Here the men stopped to drink and fill their canteens. Though this loss of time was costly, success might still have been theirs if the movement had not been detected.

From Signal Hill, a high observation point within the Manassas defenses, the Confederate signal officer, E. P. Alexander, had been scanning the horizon for any evidence of a flanking movement. With glass in hand he was examining the area in the vicinity of Sudley Ford when about 8:45 a. m. his attention was arrested by the glint of the morning sun on a brass field piece. Closer observation revealed the glitter of bayonets and musket barrels. Quickly he signaled Evans at the Stone Bridge, "Look out for your left; you are turned." This message, which was to play an important part in the tactical development of the battle,

Sudley Springs Ford, Catharpin Run. Wartime photograph. Courtesy Library of Congress.

The ruins of the Stone Bridge over Bull Run, from the east. Here opened the First Battle of Manassas. Wartime photograph. Courtesy National Archives.

represents probably the first use under combat conditions of the "wigwag" system of signaling.

MORNING PHASE—THE FIGHT AT MATTHEWS HILL. Since 8 o'clock it had been apparent to Evans that Tyler's attack was simply a feint. Now warned of the approach of the flanking column, he moved rapidly to counter it. Leaving four companies of his command to guard the bridge with two pieces of artillery, he pushed northwestward about 1,700 yards to a point near the crossing of the Warrenton Turnpike and the Manassas-Sudley Road. There, about 10:15 a. m., he opened with artillery and infantry fire upon the advancing Federal column led by Burnside's brigade. Soon Col. Andrew Porter moved to Burnside's assistance. Hard-pressed after a gallant stand of about an hour, Evans sent an urgent request to Bee for help. Temporarily attached to Bee's brigade was Bartow with two Georgia regiments. With his command Bee had previously taken up a position on Henry Hill from which point Imboden's battery had played with telling effect upon the flanking column of McDowell.

Bee moved promptly forward, taking up a position on the right of Evans' line about 11 a. m. Here the combined Confederate force of approximately five regiments with six field pieces held stubbornly until about noon. The arrival of fresh Federal reinforcements of Heintzelman, and later of Sherman and Keyes, so increased the pressure on the Confederate right that its defenses gave way. Eagerly the Federal columns pushed their advantage as the now demoralized Confederates retreated across Young's Branch to the shelter of the Robinson House Hill. Following closely, Keyes moved downstream and took up a position in the shelter of the hills where he remained to take little effective part in further fighting during the day.

In a position near the Robinson House, Hampton's Legion, 600 strong, courageously attempted to cover the Confederate retreat. The Federal attack, however, finally forced them back with the disordered commands of Bee, Bartow, and Evans.

In the midst of the wild confusion that then ensued, as the fate of the battle hung in the balance, there occurred one of the dramatic moments of the war. Bee, desperately attempting to rally his men, glanced toward Henry Hill where he saw Jackson and his command standing bold and

Confederate officers rallying their troops behind the Robinson House during

resolute. Catching the inspiration of the moment, Bee leaned forward in his stirrups and with pointed sword shouted to his men, "Look! There is Jackson standing like a stone wall! Rally behind the Virginians!" Thus "Stonewall" Jackson won his famous sobriquet.

It was about this time that Johnston and Beauregard galloped upon the field. In the presence of their commanding officers the men gained new confidence. The line stiffened, formed again, and advanced to the front. Reinforcements from Cocke's and Bonham's brigades, at fords farther down Bull Run, were now fast coming up. Quickly upon their arrival they were sent into position to the right and left of Jackson. Johnston soon retired to the Lewis House ("Portici"), where he directed the movement of reinforcements from the rear, while Beauregard took immediate command of the field.

There now occurred a lull between 1 and 2 p. m. as the victorious Federal troops crossed the valley of Young's Branch and re-formed for a renewal of the attack.

AFTERNOON PHASE. About 2 p. m., McDowell ordered forward the two splendid, regular batteries of Ricketts and Griffin, directing them to take

the First Battle of Manassas. From "Battles and Leaders of the Civil War."

up an exposed position just south of the Henry House. At a distance of not much more than 300 yards, these batteries were soon engaged in a furious duel with the artillery arrayed in Jackson's front. For about 15 minutes the din was terrific. Finally, in an effort to gain a better enfilading fire, Griffin advanced three of his guns slightly. The movement proved fatal.

At this moment J. E. B. Stuart made a dashing cavalry charge up the Manassas-Sudley Road, scattering the colorful Fire Zouaves who had been advanced to the support of Ricketts and Griffin. Almost simultaneously the 33rd Virginia regiment moved forward. Mistaken by one of the Federal officers as a battery support, it was allowed to come within 70 yards of Griffin's guns. Suddenly the regiment delivered a murderous volley, which killed most of the horses and men of both batteries. The immobilized guns were seized by the Virginians, only to be recaptured by a spirited Federal advance. In heated charges and countercharges the guns changed hands a number of times, yet neither side was able to employ them effectively. Their loss to the Federal command was irreparable.

Federal pressure now became so strong that Beauregard decided to attack. As Jackson penetrated the center of the Federal line, the Confederate right swept clear the area in the vicinity of the Robinson House. In a gallant countercharge, however, the Union brigades of Franklin, Willcox, Sherman, and Porter surged forward to reclaim the lost ground. In the attack, McDowell displayed reckless courage by climbing to the upper story of the Henry House to obtain a better view of the whole field.

The battle now raged with increasing severity as both sides fought desperately for possession of the plateau—"the key to victory." The

The Federal assault on Henry Hill in the First Battle of Manassas. From "Battles and Leaders of the Civil War."

Gen. Joseph E. Johnston in command of the Army of the Shenandoah. Courtesy National Archives.

Brig. Gen. Thomas J. "Stonewall" Jackson. Courtesy National Archives.

weight of Federal pressure upon Beauregard's left and right flanks so increased as to endanger his whole position. It was now about 3 p. m. The scorching rays of the sun beat unmercifully upon the exhausted troops as Beauregard, at this critical stage, ordered yet another general attack all along the line. Just then Fisher's 6th North Carolina regiment arrived to take position on the Confederate left. With Beauregard leading the charge, the Confederate line advanced to clear the field and regain final possession of the Henry and Robinson Houses.

Despite the loss of the plateau, McDowell's position was still strong. With his right anchored in the woods in the vicinity of the Chinn House, his line stretched in a great crescent back of the Stone House to a position near the Stone Bridge. However, the right held by Howard's brigade and Sykes' regulars had become so extended as to face almost east towards Centreville. Thus extended, it invited an attack which the Confederate command was quick to mount. Reinforcements, sent forward by Johnston, now rapidly moved up. In the lead were Kershaw's 2d and Cash's 8th South Carolina regiments followed by Kemper's battery. Quickly following these troops came Elzey's brigade, 1,700 strong. This brigade of Johnston's Army, detrained only a few hours before, had advanced to the sound of firing, led by Kirby Smith. To the weight of these numbers was added still another fresh brigade—Early's. Coming into position to the left of Elzey's brigade, Early struck the Federal right in flank and rear.

The combined attack, delivered about 3:45 p.m., proved overwhelming. The Federal line staggered and fell back, retiring across the field in some semblance of order. A brief rally north of Young's Branch was broken up by Confederate artillery fire. All other attempts to rally the men proved futile. They had had enough. Now they continued homeward by the various routes of the morning's advance. Bravely covering the retreat were Sykes' regulars and Palmer's squadron of cavalry.

As the main body of the Federal army retreated in the direction of Sudley Ford, Keyes' brigade recrossed at the Stone Bridge closely pursued by a Confederate detachment led by Kemper's battery. Riding astraddle one of the guns was the venerable "Yankee hater," Edmund Ruffin, who had fired one of the first shots at Fort Sumter. Dusty and weary he had arrived upon the field in the closing moments of the battle in time to hail Kemper's battery as it was passing. Eager to get another shot at the enemy, he held precariously to his seat as the battery went jolting past the Stone Bridge and along the pike now littered with arms, accoutrements, haversacks, knapsacks, loose articles of clothing, blankets, drums, and brass musical instruments left by the rapidly retiring troops.

After proceeding a few miles, Kemper's guns reached an advantageous rise. There they were unlimbered and quickly made ready for firing. The first shot, fired by the elderly Ruffin, hit squarely upon the suspension bridge over Cub Run upsetting a wagon that had just been driven upon it. This served to barricade the bridge to further use by other vehicles. In quick succession more shots were fired. Complete panic now seized the Federal troops as they fled in a wild rout back to Washington. Adding to the confusion were the throngs of sightseers and fugitives who crowded the narrow roads. The roar of the flight, wrote Russell, *The London Times'* correspondent, was like the rush of a great river. All

The Robinson House. From a wartime photograph in "Photographic History of the Civil War."

through the night and the rain of the next day the tide of soldiers and civilians streamed into Washington. Attempts by McDowell to rally the soldiers were in vain.

The exhausted, battle-weary Confederates made no effective pursuit. Early's brigade and Stuart's cavalry did succeed in capturing quite a number of prisoners, but the main Union force escaped. July 22 found both armies in the positions they had occupied prior to the 16th.

EFFECTS OF FIRST MANASSAS. The news of the disaster was first received in the Capital with incredulity and amazement, then with consternation. Throughout the night President Lincoln received spectators of the battle and listened in silence to their descriptions of the engagement.

"For a few days," writes Channing, "the North was dazed, stocks went down, money went up, and people sat around with their hands folded in despair. Then, almost as by magic, the scene shifted and stern resolve took the place of the hysteria of the Hundred Days since Sumter. Lincoln called for volunteers. The best blood of the North in all ranks of society, in the East, in the Ohio Valley, and on the shores of the Great Lakes responded. The new men went into the conflict with a determination and a spirit that has seldom been seen and never excelled."

In the South, the news of the victory was received with great elation. Thanksgiving sermons were preached from the pulpits while public officials commemorated the event with congratulatory proclamations. In the ill-considered opinion of many Southerners the war was over, yet seldom if ever has so complete a victory borne such meager results. An overweening confidence and a false sense of security developed in the South a paralysis of enterprise more damaging to it than was the disaster of defeat for the North.

The battle, however, as the English historian Fuller points out, was to have a profound influence on the grand strategy of the war. "First, it imbued the Southern politicians with an exaggerated idea of the prowess of their soldiers and so led them to under-estimate the fighting capacity of their enemy; secondly, it so terrified Lincoln and his Government that from now onwards until 1864, east of the Alleghanies, the defence of Washington became the pivot of Northern strategy."

Though the men of each army had fought with flashes of steadiness and exceptional courage, there was ample evidence to show the costly result of inadequate training.

	FEDERAL	CONFEDERATE
Strength, approximate	35,000	32,000
CASUALTIES		
Killed	460	387
Wounded	1,124	1,582
Captured or missing	1,312	13
Total	2,896	1,982

Winter's Lull

Following the conclusion of the first Manassas campaign, the war in Virginia "languished" until the spring of 1862. The North, smarting from the humiliating defeat suffered at Bull Run, now turned with grim determination to the mobilization of its resources and to the training of the great land forces necessary to subjugate the South. Maj. Gen. George B. McClellan, fresh from victories in western Virginia, was immediately called to the command of the Federal forces around Washington. Soldierly in bearing and engaging in manner, McClellan proved a popular choice with the Nation and the army. With marked success he initiated a program of organization and training of the great Army of the Potomac. Recruits now streamed into Washington by the thousand. By December, there were 150,000 in training; by spring, over 200,000.

Meanwhile, the Confederate army under Joseph E. Johnston remained encamped at Centreville with outposts along the Potomac. Jackson, with a detachment, was stationed at Winchester. It was during this time that Johnston established a very strongly fortified position consisting of an L-shaped line of earthwork forts and batteries connected by infantry trenches that extended along the eastern and northern crests of Centreville for a distance of approximately 5 miles. Gradually, on the approach of winter, log or board huts were constructed for winter quarters for the troops. These were so located as to permit the troops easy access to the fortifications.

With the worsening condition of the roads the problem of supply became increasingly difficult. It was then that Johnston built a branch

Quaker guns at Centreville. Confederate winter quarters are shown in background. Wartime photograph. Courtesy National Archives.

railroad from his base at Manassas Junction. This was one of the first railroads ever to be used solely for military purposes.

Preliminary Operations to Second Manassas

McClellan's failure to move against Johnston resulted in a restive public and press. Richmond, rather than Centreville, now became the immediate Federal objective. Learning of an anticipated movement against Richmond via Urbanna, Johnston, on March 9, fell back from Centreville to take up a position south of the Rappahannock, with his right resting at Fredericksburg and his left at Culpeper Court House. This forced a modification of McClellan's original plan. He thereupon decided to make the movement by water to Fortress Monroe and from there advance up the Peninsula upon Richmond.

On March 17, the Federal army embarked from Alexandria. McClellan had anticipated the use of a force of about 155,000 men. The brilliant operations of "Stonewall" Jackson in the Shenandoah Valley during the next 3 months, however, so alarmed President Lincoln as to cause him to immobilize nearly 40,000 of McDowell's troops at Fredericksburg to secure the defenses of Washington. This, together with the detention of Banks' expected reinforcements in the Valley, reduced McClellan's force to approximately 100,000, thereby materially minimizing his chances of success. Seldom has so small a force as that of Jackson (approximately 16,000) so largely influenced the final outcome of a major military operation.

Johnston, in the meantime, had reinforced Magruder at Yorktown. On May 4 the town was evacuated, and the next day a successful rearguard action was fought at Williamsburg, covering the Confederate withdrawal to Richmond. The Federal army followed by land and water to White House on the Pamunkey where, on May 16, McClellan set up his headquarters. The next day the Federal forces resumed their advance on Richmond.

Gathering a force of some 63,000 men, Johnston then determined to attack. On May 31, in the Battle of Seven Pines, followed by the Battle of Fair Oaks the next day, the Confederates were repulsed, and Johnston was severely wounded. The command of the Army of Northern Virginia now devolved upon Robert E. Lee, a command that he was not to relinquish until the end of the war. Within 2 weeks the defenses of Richmond had been strengthened and the morale of the troops greatly improved.

By June 25, Lee had assembled a force of about 90,000 men, including Jackson's victorious command from the Valley. The next day he launched his great counteroffensive. In a series of desperately contested operations, known as the Seven Days' Battles before Richmond, McClellan was forced back upon Harrison's Landing on the James. Though the cam-

Maj. Gen. John Pope, in command of the Federal Army, Second Battle of Manassas. Courtesy National Archives.

Gen. Robert E. Lee, in command of the Army of Northern Virginia. Courtesy National Archives.

paign was costly in Confederate casualties, Lee saved Richmond and cloaked his army with a sense of invincibility.

Pope Concentrates Behind the Rapidan

The failure of Fremont, Banks, and McDowell in the Shenandoah Valley convinced President Lincoln of the desirability of consolidating their armies under a single head. By order of June 26 the "Army of Virginia" was created, and Maj. Gen. John Pope, who had won recent successes in the West, was given the command. Shortly thereafter, Gen. Henry W. Halleck was recalled from the West to be made general in chief of the Federal armies.

To Pope was entrusted the responsibility for covering Washington, protecting the Shenandoah Valley, and so operating against the Confederate communications at Gordonsville and Charlottesville as to draw off heavy detachments from Richmond, thereby relieving the pressure on McClellan. On July 14, Pope ordered an advance on Gordonsville. Lee, anticipating the movement, had ordered Jackson to this point the day before.

On August 7, Jackson, having been reinforced by A. P. Hill, moved toward Culpeper in the hope of capturing the town and using it in a series of operations against Pope. Two days later he fell upon Banks at Cedar Mountain in a sharp but indecisive encounter.

Lee now learned that McClellan had been ordered to evacuate the Peninsula and reinforce Pope. Appreciating the necessity of striking Pope before he could be joined by such heavy reinforcements, Lee moved with Longstreet's corps to reinforce Jackson. Pope's force now numbered about 47,000 effectives, while Lee had approximately 55,000.

Lee's Operations Along the Rapidan and Rappahannock

Pope's center was now at Cedar Mountain, his right at Robertson's River, and his left near Raccoon Ford on the Rapidan. Thus stationed, his army was directly opposite Gordonsville where Jackson's force had recently arrived. On Clark's Mountain (a high hill opposite Pope's left) the Confederates had established a signal station. From here, stretching for miles, could be seen the white tents of the Federal encampment dotting the Culpeper tablelands. Spurs from Clark's Mountain paralleled the Rapidan to Somerville Ford, located about 2 miles from Raccoon Ford.

Lee was quick to appreciate the advantage this topography afforded him. Massing his troops behind Clark's Mountain he might move under its protecting screen, fall upon Pope's left at Somerville Ford, and cut off his retreat to Washington. The opportunity held bright possibilities of success, and August 18 was set as the date for the initiation of the movement. Unforeseen delays postponed the movement until the 20th. Worse still for the Confederates, Stuart's adjutant general was captured, bearing a copy of Lee's order.

Thus warned, Pope withdrew his army behind the Rappahannock. Lee followed closely on the 20th, crossing to the north side of the river. Pope took up an advantageous position where he stood fast during 5 days of feints and demonstrations as Lee sought eagerly for an opening on the right. In the meantime, Stuart had captured Pope's headquarters. Thus, Lee learned that 20,000 troops, composing the corps of Heintzelman and Porter and the division of Reynolds, were within 2 days' march of the front. Within 5 days other expected reinforcements would swell Pope's numbers to about 130,000 men.

The situation was so desperate as to demand a bold expedient. Quickly, Lee made his decision. Jackson, with Stuart's cavalry comprising about 24,000 men, was to be sent on a wide flanking movement of Pope's right for the purpose of destroying his communications with Washington.

Map

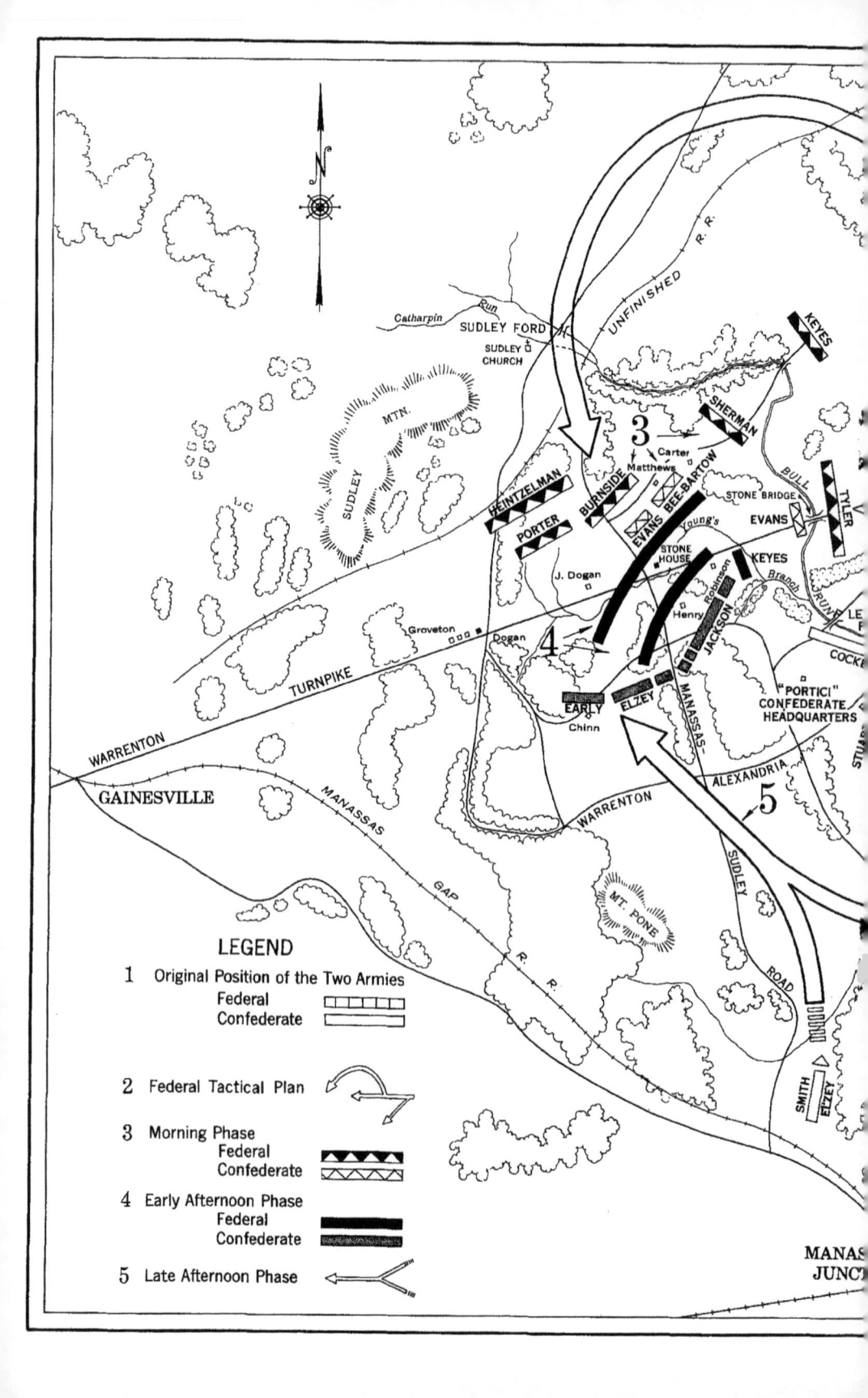

Locations: Catharpin Run, Sudley Ford, Sudley Church, Sudley Mtn., Unfinished R.R., Matthews, Carter, Stone Bridge, Young's Branch, Stone House, J. Dogan, Groveton, Dogan, Henry, Robinson, Chinn, "Portici" Confederate Headquarters, Bull Run, Cocke, Mt. Pone, Warrenton Turnpike, Gainesville, Manassas Gap R.R., Warrenton, Sudley Road, Manassas-Alexandria R.R., Manassas Junction

Units: Keyes, Sherman, Tyler, Evans, Heintzelman, Burnside, Porter, Evans, Bee-Bartow, Keyes, Jackson, Early, Elzey, Smith, Elzey

LEGEND

1. Original Position of the Two Armies
   - Federal
   - Confederate

2. Federal Tactical Plan

3. Morning Phase
   - Federal
   - Confederate

4. Early Afternoon Phase
   - Federal
   - Confederate

5. Late Afternoon Phase

THE BATTLE OF FIRST MANASSAS
July 21, 1861

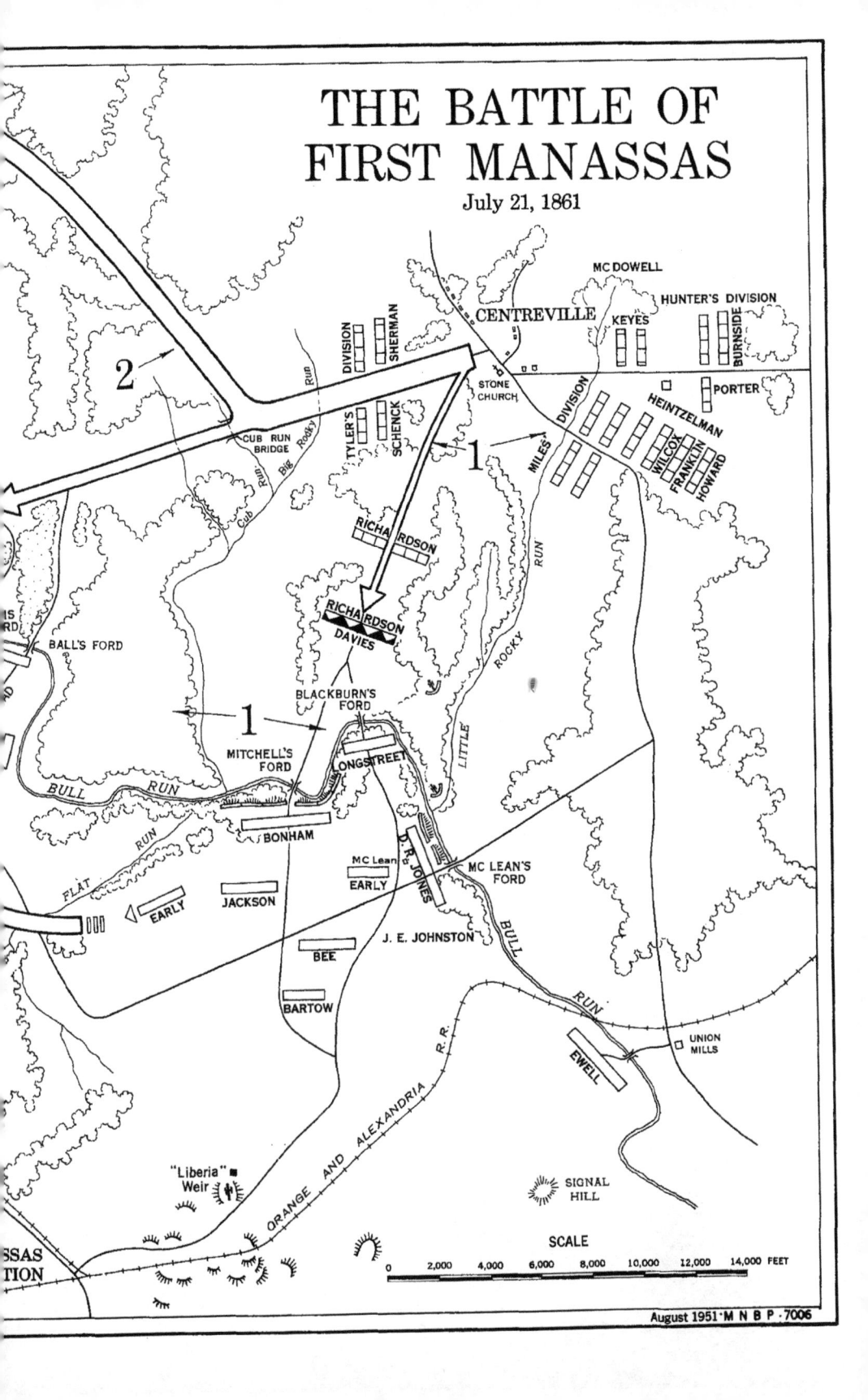

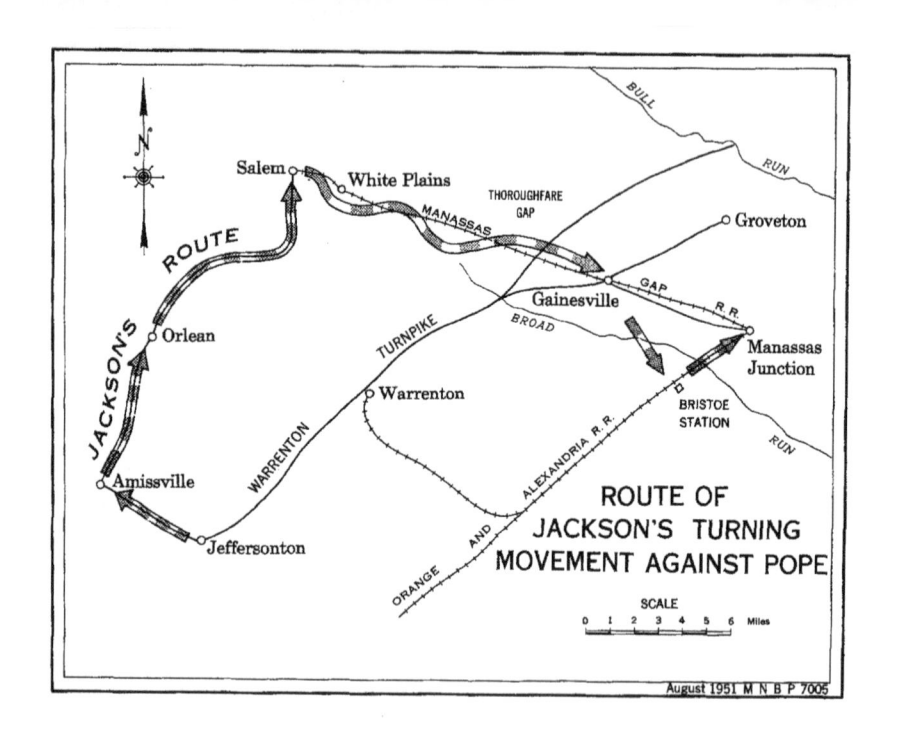

ROUTE OF JACKSON'S TURNING MOVEMENT AGAINST POPE

Commenting on this decision, Henderson, the English biographer of Jackson, says "we have record of few enterprises of greater daring."

With Lee and Longstreet covering the line of the Rappahannock, Jackson began his march from Jeffersonton on August 25. He moved through Amissville and Orlean to bivouac that night at Salem. The next day he pushed on past Thoroughfare Gap and Gainesville to Bris-

Jackson and his foot cavalry. From the painting by Hoffbauer in Battle Abbey, Richmond, Va. Courtesy Virginia Historical Society.

Jackson's troops pillaging Federal supplies at Manassas Junction just prior to the Second Battle of Manassas. From "Battles and Leaders of the Civil War."

toe. Never did the "foot cavalry" better deserve its name, for in 2 days it had covered approximately 51 miles. That night Jackson sent Stuart and two regiments to Manassas Junction to capture Pope's great base of supplies. The task was accomplished with little effort.

The next day Jackson left Ewell to cover the rear at Bristoe and moved with the rest of his command to Manassas Junction. There then fol-

Manassas Junction, Va., as it looked after Jackson's raid. Wartime photograph. Courtesy National Archives.

lowed a scene of feasting and plunder the like of which has seldom been witnessed. Knapsacks, haversacks, and canteens were filled with articles of every description. Added to vast quantities of quartermaster and commissary supplies were innumerable luxuries from sutler stores, including expensive liquors and imported wines. An eyewitness writes, "To see a starving man eating lobster salad & drinking rhine wine, barefooted & in tatters was curious; the whole thing is indescribable." What could not be eaten or carried away was finally put to the torch. With the destruction of these supplies one of the chief objectives of the campaign had been accomplished.

Second Battle of Manassas (SEE MAP ON PAGES 28–29.)

FIRST PHASE—BRISTOE AND MANASSAS, AUGUST 27. Pope, now advised of the presence of Jackson in his rear, immediately ordered a concentration of his forces in order to crush him. McDowell's and Sigel's corps, together with the division of Reynolds, were to move to Gainesville, while Reno's corps, with Kearny's division of Heintzelman's corps, was to concentrate at Greenwich. By these dispositions Pope hoped to intercept any reinforcements coming to Jackson by way of Thoroughfare Gap. With Hooker's division of Heintzelman's corps Pope moved along the railroad to Manassas Junction.

On the afternoon of August 27, Hooker attacked Ewell and drove him back upon Bristoe. During the night, Ewell retired to Manassas where he joined the rest of Jackson's force. Pope now learned for the first time that the whole of Jackson's command was at Manassas. New orders were issued for a concentration at that point. Porter was ordered to march at 1 a.m. of the 28th from Warrenton Junction and be in position at Bristoe by daylight. McDowell, Sigel, and Reno were to move at dawn upon Manassas Junction, while Kearny was to advance at the same hour upon Bristoe.

About 3 a.m., August 28, Jackson began to move out of Manassas toward Groveton. In order to mystify and mislead Pope, he sent Taliaferro along the Manassas-Sudley Road, Ewell along the Centreville Road via Blackburn's Ford and the Stone Bridge to Groveton, and A. P. Hill to Centreville and thence along the Warrenton Pike to a position near Sudley Church.

Moving with Kearny's division, Pope arrived at Manassas Junction at noon, to find the town deserted. Later in the day, word was received that the Confederates had been seen in Centreville. Pope thereupon ordered a concentration at this place in the belief that Jackson's whole force was there. The corps of Heintzelman and Reno moved along the Centreville Road; Sigel and Reynolds along the Manassas-Sudley Road; King's division of McDowell's corps along the Warrenton Pike.

Longstreet's troops skirmishing at Thoroughfare Gap. From "Manassas to Appomattox."

SECOND PHASE—GROVETON, AUGUST 28. Jackson had but a short time before concentrated north of the turnpike when word was received that King's Federal column was approaching from Gainesville. There was now need for a quick decision. To allow King to pass unmolested would defeat the purpose of the campaign by permitting Pope to assume an impregnable position on the heights at Centreville. To attack, without assurance as to when Longstreet would arrive, was to invite the assault of Pope's whole force with possible fatal consequences. Without hesitation he ordered the divisions of Taliaferro and Ewell to advance. A fierce and stubborn fight ensued which resulted in heavy losses on both sides. Finally, about 9 p. m., King withdrew towards Manassas.

In the meantime, Longstreet had reached Thoroughfare Gap at about 3 p. m. of the same day to find his way blocked by Federal troops under Ricketts. Outmaneuvering his opponent by way of Hopewell Gap, he forced him to fall back to Gainesville. That night, without informing Pope of their intentions, King and Ricketts decided to move towards Manassas. This enabled Longstreet to effect an easy junction with Jackson in the afternoon of the following day.

THIRD PHASE—MAIN BATTLE, AUGUST 29-30. When Pope learned of the engagement of Groveton he mistakenly decided that King had met the head of Jackson's column in retreat. Confident of success, he ordered a concentration of his leg weary troops to crush the Confederate force. Sigel and Reynolds were to attack at dawn, reinforced by Heintzelman and Reno. McDowell and Porter were ordered to reverse their course and push toward Gainesville in an effort to cut off Jackson's retreat.

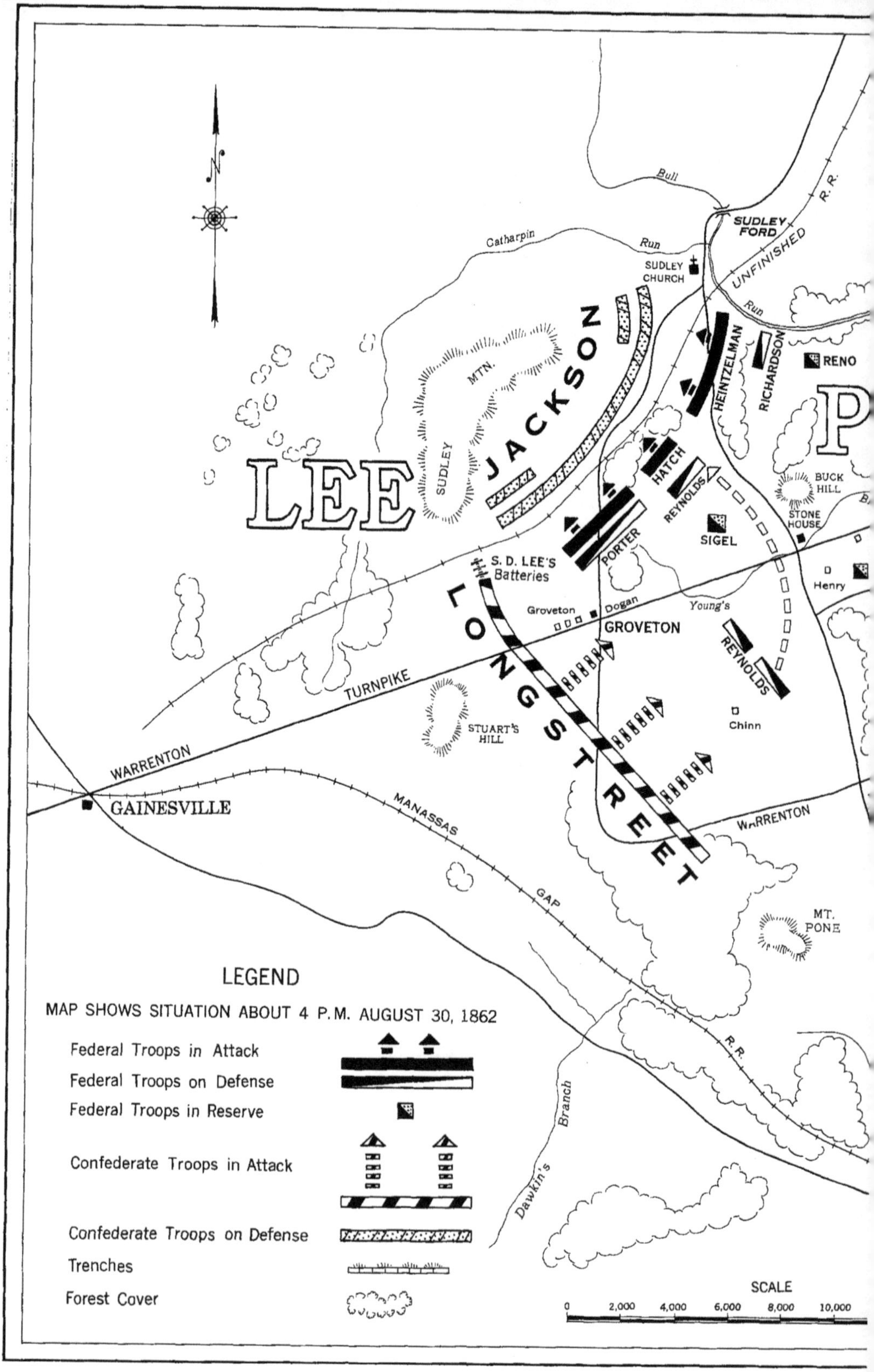

LEE
JACKSON
LONGSTREET
P
Bull
Run
Catharpin
Run
SUDLEY FORD
SUDLEY CHURCH
UNFINISHED
R.R.
Run
HEINTZELMAN
RICHARDSON
RENO
SUDLEY
MTN.
HATCH
REYNOLDS
BUCK HILL
STONE HOUSE
SIGEL
PORTER
S. D. LEE'S Batteries
Henry
Groveton
Dogan
Young's
GROVETON
REYNOLDS
Chinn
TURNPIKE
WARRENTON
STUART'S HILL
GAINESVILLE
MANASSAS
GAP
R.R.
WARRENTON
MT. PONE
Dawkin's Branch
LEGEND
MAP SHOWS SITUATION ABOUT 4 P.M. AUGUST 30, 1862
Federal Troops in Attack
Federal Troops on Defense
Federal Troops in Reserve
Confederate Troops in Attack
Confederate Troops on Defense
Trenches
Forest Cover
SCALE
0 2,000 4,000 6,000 8,000 10,000

THE BATTLE OF SECOND MANASSAS
AUGUST 29-30, 1862

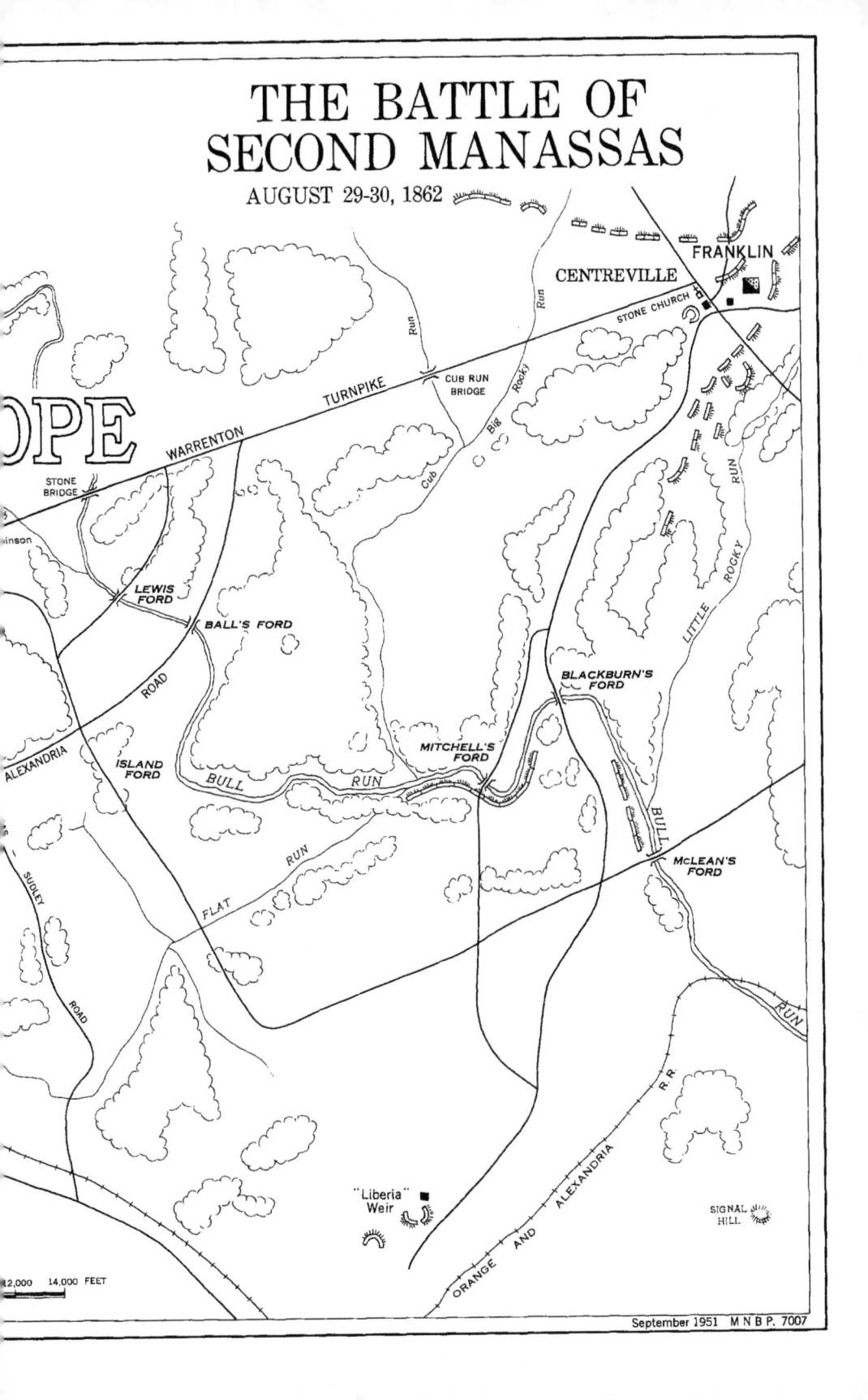

The text of this order known as the "Joint Order," which was received about noon, reads as follows:

> HEADQUARTERS ARMY OF VIRGINIA
> *Centreville, August 29, 1862.*
>
> Generals McDowell and Porter:
>
> You will please move forward with your joint commands toward Gainesville. I sent General Porter written orders to that effect an hour and a half ago. Heintzelman, Sigel, and Reno are moving on the Warrenton turnpike, and must now be not far from Gainesville. I desire that as soon as communication is established between this force and your own the whole command shall halt. It may be necessary to fall back behind Bull Run at Centreville to-night. I presume it will be so, on account of our supplies. . . .
>
> If any considerable advantages are to be gained by departing from this order it will not be strictly carried out. One thing must be had in view, that the troops must occupy a position from which they can reach Bull Run to-night or by morning. The indications are that the whole force of the enemy is moving in this direction at a pace that will bring them here by to-morrow night or the next day. My own headquarters will be for the present with Heintzelman's corps or at this place.
>
> Jno. Pope,
> *Major-General, Commanding.*

Prior to the receipt of the "Joint Order," Porter had reversed his course to Centreville and had moved as far as Dawkin's Branch, located about 3 miles from Gainesville. Finding the Confederates strongly posted in his front, he deployed a brigade of his leading division and waited. McDowell, who arrived shortly thereafter, showed him a dispatch he had received a few minutes before from Buford, who commanded the Union cavalry on the right. The dispatch stated that 17 regiments, 1 battery, and 500 cavalry had passed through Gainesville about 8:45 a. m. This was the advance of Longstreet's command which had left Thoroughfare Gap early that morning and now, followed by heavy reinforcements, was moving into position on Jackson's right (Porter's front).

This information, the generals felt, had not reached Pope. After a conference, it was decided that in face of this new development they would take advantage of the latitude the order granted: McDowell would move towards Groveton, while Porter would remain in the vicinity of his present position.

The relative quiet in this sector was in sharp contrast to the heavy fighting now taking place along Jackson's front. With about 18,000 infantry and 40 guns, Jackson had taken up a position along an unfinished railroad bed which extended from near Sudley Springs 2 miles southwesterly to Groveton. The grades and cuts of this road provided ready-made entrenchments and formed a very strong position. There, shortly after sunrise, Sigel's and Reynolds' columns were seen at a distance deploying for the attack. About 7 a. m., the Federal batteries opened fire.

Maj. Gen. Fitz-John Porter, in command of the Fifth Army Corps at the Second Battle of Manassas. Courtesy Library of Congress.

By 10:30 a. m., a number of sharp skirmishes had taken place, but no general assault had been made. About this time Federal reinforcements of Reno and Kearny reached the field. It was not until 2 p. m., however, that the battle reached its height. All afternoon in violent but uncoordinated attacks, blue columns gallantly assaulted Jackson's line. At one point the Confederate left was pushed back dangerously near the breaking point, but the gray line steadied and held. Towards dusk, King's division, of McDowell's corps, arrived in time to take part in the action, engaging a part of Longstreet's command which was then advancing on a reconnaissance.

Pope, still unaware of the arrival of Longstreet on the field, late in the day sent Porter the following order to attack Jackson's right at once:

HEADQUARTERS IN THE FIELD,
August 29–4:30 p. m.

Major-General Porter:

Your line of march brings you in on the enemy's right flank. I desire you to push forward into action at once on the enemy's flank, and, if possible, on his rear, keeping your right in communication with General Reynolds. The enemy is massed in the woods in front of us, but can be shelled out as soon as you engage their flank. Keep heavy reserves and use your batteries, keeping well closed to your right all the time. In case you are obliged to fall back, do so to your right and rear, so as to keep you in close communication with the right wing.

John Pope,
Major-General, Commanding.

This order, dated 4:30 p. m., was received by Porter at Bethlehem Church about 6:30 p. m. Upon receipt of the order Porter immediately sent his chief of staff, Locke, to order Morell's division to attack. Shortly thereafter Porter rode to the front to find Morell's preparations for the attack complete. By this time, however, it was so late that Porter decided to rescind the order.[1]

During the night the Confederates retired from the advanced positions gained during the day to their original battleline. This fact was reported from the field early on the morning of the 30th and later confirmed by a reconnaissance by McDowell and Heintzelman. This led Pope falsely to assume that Lee was in retreat to Thoroughfare Gap. Immediately, plans were initiated to press a vigorous pursuit. At midday the following order was issued:

> Special Orders,   HEADQUARTERS NEAR GROVETON,
> No. —   *August* 30, 1862—12 M.
>
> The following forces will be immediately thrown forward and in pursuit of the enemy, and press him vigorously during the whole day. Major-General McDowell is assigned to the command of the pursuit.
>
> Major-General Porter's corps will push forward on the Warrenton turnpike, followed by the divisions of Brigadier-Generals King and Reynolds. The division of Brigadier-General Ricketts will pursue the Hay Market road, followed by the corps of Major-General Heintzelman. . . .

At 3 a. m. of the 30th, Porter received Pope's dispatch ordering him to march his command immediately to the field of battle of the previous day. In compliance with this order he promptly withdrew from his position facing Longstreet and marched rapidly along the Sudley Road to the center of the battlefield where he reported to Pope for orders. Though this movement strengthened the center, it dangerously weakened the Federal left.

From its contracted left near Groveton, the Federal line now extended approximately 3 miles to Bull Run near Sudley Church. The opposing Confederate line was about 4 miles long. Jackson held the left along the unfinished railroad, while Longstreet held the right, with the main body of his troops "bent to the front" south of the Warrenton Pike. A heavy concentration of artillery was placed on high ground between the two wings. These guns commanded the open fields and the stretch of woods near Jackson's right and center.

---

[1] For his failure to carry out Pope's order of the 29th to attack Jackson, Porter was court-martialed and dismissed from the army on January 21, 1863. In 1879, a board of general officers who reviewed the case held that Porter could not have attacked Jackson successfully, as ordered, because Longstreet's corps had moved up into position on the right of Jackson and opposite Porter, and that this was known to the latter. Thus, Pope's order, which was written without knowledge of this development, could not be carried out. President Arthur, in 1882, remitted that part of the sentence which disqualified Porter from holding any office of trust or profit under the Government of the United States. On August 5, 1886, Porter was reappointed colonel of infantry, and 2 days later placed on the retirement list. To this day, despite his final vindication, the controversy over Porter's action on August 29, 1862, at Second Manassas has not died down among military students.

Preparations completed about midafternoon, the Federal columns of Porter and Heintzelman advanced three lines deep, preceded by a swarm of skirmishers and supported by great masses of men and guns in the rear. A strange quiet pervaded the fields as the unsuspecting troops pushed forward. Behind their protective cover, the Confederates watched the lines draw closer; then suddenly opened upon them a rapid artillery fire. Instantly, the infantry bugles sounded the alarm alerting Jackson's men to action. The Federal advance line halted and staggered back. Other brigades quickly pushed forward only to be broken by the raking force of the fire.

Soon it was apparent that the main Federal assault was being directed by Porter and Hatch against Jackson's right and center held by the divisions of Starke and Lawton. In gallant style, a third line moved up and impetuously pressed the attack. The force of this forward movement pushed back the famous Stonewall brigade, but later it reestablished its lines in a desperate countercharge. Heavy fighting at close quarters now ensued. At one point in their line near a section of the railroad bed known as the "Deep Cut," Jackson's veterans, with ammunition exhausted, partially repelled an attack with stones from the embankment.

Some of Jackson's Confederates, their ammunition exhausted, hurling rocks at the advancing Federals, during the Second Battle of Manassas. From "Battles and Leaders of the Civil War."

Finally, the pressure became so great that Jackson sent an urgent request for reinforcements. Lee then ordered forward a brigade from Longstreet's command. Anticipating the request, Longstreet had already moved up the batteries of Stephen D. Lee, which now opened a withering fire on the Federal columns on Jackson's right and center. The effect was devastating. Within 15 minutes the whole aspect of the battle had changed.

Shortly after the Federal brigades had engaged Jackson along the unfinished railroad, Pope had ordered Reynolds' division from his left at Bald Hill to move up and support the attack on the right. The weight of his numbers, however, proved insufficient to stem the tide of retreat that had now set in. Quickly, Jackson ordered up two brigades to press a counterattack, moving forward his artillery as the infantry advanced.

The transfer of Reynolds' division had again greatly weakened the Federal left. Lee saw this and realized that here at last was the opportunity for which he had been waiting. The order was sent immediately to Longstreet to deliver the counterstroke. Every regiment, battery, and squadron of both wings of the army were to be employed. By sheer weight of numbers the attack was to be driven home in successive waves of assault, piling one upon the other.

"The battle of Groveton or Second Bull Run between the Union Army commanded by Genl. Pope and Con. Army under Genl. Robert E. Lee. Sketched from Bald face hill (Henry Hill) on Saturday afternoon half past three o'clock . . . Looking toward the village of Groveton." From original wartime sketch, with title by E. Forbes. Courtesy Library of Congress.

Again, Longstreet had anticipated the order for which he had been preparing since dawn. The long gray lines of infantry, restive for the fray, now swept forward in a furious assault. In advance came Hood's Texans, their colors gleaming red in the evening sun. Above the thunderous roar of artillery and the noise of battle could be heard the shrill cries of the rebel yell echoing through the Groveton valley. So intense was the excitement that only with the greatest difficulty could the officers restrain their men. Rapidly moving up in support came the divisions of Anderson, Kemper, and D. R. Jones. Across the rolling fields the attack pushed to gain the promontory of Chinn Ridge despite a stubborn defense by the Union brigades of McLean, Tower, and Milroy, while Jackson's veterans successfully assailed Buck Hill.

On Henry Hill, poignant with memories of the previous year, were now assembled Reynolds' divisions, Sykes' regulars, and other available troops. With courage and gallantry that matched the crisis of battle, they hurled back repeated Confederate assaults that continued until dark. The successful defense of Henry Hill made possible Pope's retreat over

Note. The artist identified the following points:
"1. *Thoroughfare Gap through which Genl. Lee's Army passed.*
2. *Rebs line of battle.*
3. *The old R.R. embankment behind which the Con. were posted.*
4. *The old Stone House on the Turnpike used as a hospital.*
5. *Warrenton Turnpike.*
6. *Bald face hill {Henry Hill}.*
7. *Henry Hill {Buck Hill}.*
8. *Union line of battle.*
9. *McDowell's corps moving to the left flank to repel Longstreet's attack which had just commenced.*
10. *Sudley Springs road."*

The "Deep Cut" where Porter's troops made a gallant bid for victory. Here a Federal flag held its position for half an hour within 10 yards of a Confederate regimental flag. Six times it fell, only to be raised again. From "Battles and Leaders of the Civil War."

Bull Run, by the Stone Bridge and other fords, to the strong defenses of the Centreville plateau.

FOURTH PHASE—CHANTILLY, SEPTEMBER 1. Considering the Centreville position as unfavorable for attack, Lee sent Jackson by Sudley Ford to the Little River Turnpike in an effort to turn the Federal right and threaten communications with Washington. The movement, however, was anticipated by Pope, and the divisions of Stevens and Kearny were sent to check it. In a sharp contest, fought in a rainstorm at Chantilly on September 1, Stevens and Kearny were killed; but Jackson was repulsed. During the next 2 days Pope retired to the defenses of Washington.

The Federal retreat over the Stone Bridge on Saturday evening, August 30, 1862. From "Battles and Leaders of the Civil War."

Ruins of the Henry House after the Second Battle of Manassas.
Wartime photograph. Courtesy National Archives.

RESULTS OF SECOND BATTLE OF MANASSAS. Second Manassas offers an interesting contrast to the opening battle which had found two armies of raw, undisciplined volunteers courageously but falteringly battling for supremacy. The raw volunteers had now been replaced by seasoned veterans, hardened by months of strenuous campaigning. The campaign just ended had been one to test to the utmost the endurance and discipline of the men in the ranks of both armies—a test they had met with valor and high honor. In contrast to the rout of First Manassas, the Federal army which now retired upon Washington was a weary but defiant fighting machine. Its defeat had been accomplished by exceptional daring, combined with a skillful coordination of Confederate commands. Gambling with long chances, Lee had succeeded in removing some 150,000 invading troops from deep in Virginia and reversing the threat of impending attack upon the opposing capital.

Commenting upon the battle, Henderson, the English soldier and historian, writes:

> ... If, as Moltke avers, the junction of two armies on the field of battle is the highest achievement of military genius, the campaign against Pope has seldom been surpassed; and the great counter-stroke at Manassas is sufficient in itself to make Lee's reputation as a tactician.
> ... It was not due to the skill of Lee that Pope weakened his left at the crisis of battle. But in the rapidity with which the opportunity was seized, in the combination of the three arms, and in the vigour of the blow, Manassas is in no way inferior to Austerlitz or Salamanca.

This brilliant success did much to offset Confederate reverses in the West—the loss of Missouri, the defeats of Forts Henry and Donelson,

Shiloh, and the fall of Nashville, New Orleans, and Memphis. Contrary to the inactivity that followed First Manassas, Lee pressed his victory by the first invasion of the North. On September 4, he began moving his troops across the Potomac with the hope of winning the support of Maryland and possibly the recognition of the Confederacy by foreign powers. In the desperately fought battle of Antietam, September 17, at Sharpsburg, Md., however, these hopes were dashed by McClellan, now returned to Federal command.

	FEDERAL	CONFEDERATE
Strength	73,000 (*approx.*)	55,000
CASUALTIES		
Killed	1,747	1,553
Wounded	8,452	7,812
Captured or missing	4,263	109
Total	14,462	9,474

The War After Second Manassas

From Antietam, Lee retired to Virginia. With the coming of winter snows he bloodily repelled Maj. Gen. Ambrose E. Burnside in the Battle of Fredericksburg, December 13, 1862. In the spring, Confederate arms achieved brilliant success in the defeat of Maj. Gen. Joseph E. Hooker in the Battle of Chancellorsville, May 1-6, 1863. Capitalizing on his victory, Lee again invaded the North. At Gettysburg, July 1-3, he was defeated by Maj. Gen. George Gordon Meade. The next day saw the end of one of the most brilliant and decisive operations of the war with the surrender of Vicksburg to Maj. Gen. Ulysses S. Grant. Its fall cut the Confederacy in two and opened the Mississippi to Federal commerce and control. From the telling force of these simultaneous blows the Confederacy never recovered.

On March 9, 1864, Grant was placed in supreme command of all Federal armies. Now as never before, the full strength and resources of the republic were marshalled for a great offensive to be delivered simultaneously on all fronts. Attaching himself to Meade's army, Grant crossed the Rapidan on May 4 to launch his overland campaign against Richmond, while Sherman began the famous march that was to carry him to Atlanta and the sea.

In the fiercely contested battles of the Wilderness and Spotsylvania Court House, May 5-6 and 8-21, respectively, Grant largely succeeded in destroying Lee's offensive power, forcing his retirement upon Richmond. Repulsed with heavy losses at Cold Harbor, June 3, Grant moved upon Petersburg again to encounter Lee's army.

Ten months of siege followed as Grant methodically cut the Confed-

View northwest across Henry Hill. The present Henry House is seen in center background.

erate lifeline. On April 2, Lee evacuated Petersburg with the hope of reaching the Danville railroad and possibly effecting a junction with Johnston's forces in North Carolina. Grant's pursuit, however, was rapid and relentless. The cutting of the escape route by the Danville line and the disastrous defeat of a large segment of his army in the Battle of Sayler's Creek forced Lee to move farther westward to Appomattox Court House. There at dusk, April the 8th, the widening circle of Federal campfires brought realization that the end had been reached. The next day Lee surrendered to the magnanimous terms of Grant. On April 26, Johnston yielded to Sherman and by June all isolated units of the Confederate forces had laid down their arms.

Guide to the Area (SEE MAP ON PAGE 48.)

This guide has been prepared to enable you to identify and appreciate the chief points of historical interest on the two battlefields. While there are other locations of importance on park property and on privately owned adjacent lands, those listed below may be considered the most conspicuous.

Wherever an area, such as Henry Hill and Chinn Ridge, featured prominently in both battles, its story has been told jointly, rather than separately. This has been done in order to avoid unnecessary backtrack-

Looking west across Henry Hill to the Visitor Center. The Jackson Monument is shown in the left foreground.

ing. It should be observed that the numbers 1 to 9 have been located on a tour map for your convenience.

For the purposes of orientation a visit to the museum should precede a tour of the fields.

1. HENRY HILL. Covering an area of approximately 200 acres, the top of this plateau embraces parts of the old Henry Farm and of the Robinson tract. It extends roughly northeast from the Henry woods to Lee Highway near the site of the Robinson House. Twice the hill held the key to victory. After hours of heavy fighting in the first battle, its loss to McDowell proved a significant factor in the collapse of Federal resistance, while in the second, its stubborn defense secured the retreat of Pope's Army over Bull Run.

Some of the points of special interest here include:

Visitor Center. On a commanding rise of the hill is located the Visitor Center, which represents the focal center in the interpretation of the area. From the terrace on the north and east sides of the building, a sweeping panoramic view may be had of the valley of Young's Branch and the hills beyond which constitute the chief scenes of tactical maneuver of the two battles.

Jackson Monument. Located approximately 125 yards east of the Visitor Center is the equestrian statue of "Stonewall" Jackson. It was erected by the State of Virginia in 1940, reputedly on the spot where he received his famous nickname. To a large degree Jackson's character and personality dominated the fighting of both First and Second Manassas.

Line of Confederate Batteries. Just north of Jackson's statue are markers indicating the position of Confederate batteries of 26 guns which engaged the 11 guns of Ricketts' and Griffin's Federal batteries at a distance of about 330 yards. With this furious artillery duel the first battle reached its crisis. Today, cannon mark this position.

Bee Monument. South of the Jackson statue, about 100 feet, stands a white marble monument erected to the memory of Gen. Barnard E. Bee, who fell mortally wounded at this spot in the first battle. Shortly before, while desperately attempting to rally his men, Bee had won immortal fame with the stirring battle cry which gave Jackson the name of "Stonewall."

Bartow Monument. About 180 feet north of the Jackson statue is a stone block bearing a bronze tablet erected to the memory of Col. F. S. Bartow, commander of the 2d brigade of Johnston's army, who was killed in the first battle on this spot. At a critical moment in the early phase of the battle, Bee and Bartow had given Evans valiant support.

Position of Ricketts' and Griffin's Guns. Just south of the Henry House are cannon and markers indicating the advanced position occupied by the Union batteries of Ricketts and Griffin during the first battle. In a surprise attack, which practically annihilated these two gallant batteries, Ricketts was severely wounded.

Henry House. About 650 feet northwest of the Visitor Center stands the Henry House which was erected shortly after the war on the site of

Diorama in the museum depicting incident when Jackson was given the name "Stonewall."

the famous original structure. During the first battle, the original little house was caught in the line of cross artillery fire which killed its owner. Mrs. Judith Henry. Badly damaged, it suffered further mutilation during the following year. By the end of the second battle the house was a complete ruin.

Grave of Judith Henry. In the Henry yard, a few feet west of the house, is the grave of the widow, Judith Henry, enclosed by an iron railing and shrubbery. She is said to have been buried here by Confederate soldiers the day after the first battle. A son and daughter are also interred here. Mrs. Henry's tragic death is dramatically treated in Stephen Vincent Benet's poem, "John Brown's Body."

Union Monument. This pyramidal monument of reddish brown stone, located in the yard on the east side of the Henry House, was erected by Union soldiers in 1865 to the memory of their comrades who fell in the first battle. It is one of the earliest memorial monuments of the Civil War.

2. ROBINSON HOUSE. About 800 yards northeast of the Visitor Center, on a projecting spur, stands the Robinson House on the site of the wartime structure owned by the free Negro, James Robinson. No part of the present house is original, though a section of it dates to about 1888. The original house was torn down in 1926 to permit the construction of the larger portion of the present structure. Suffering little damage in the first battle, the original house and fields were sacked by Sigel's Federal troops in the second battle. For these damages Robinson was awarded $1,249 by Congress in a Private Act of March 3, 1873. A picturesque view unfolds from this point eastward across Bull Run and westward to the mountains.

3. STONE BRIDGE. The Stone Bridge and the stream, Bull Run, that flows beneath it are inseparably linked with the story of the two battles

The Stone Bridge as it now appears.

of Manassas. Located on the Warrenton Turnpike, approximately 1½ miles east of its intersection with the Manassas-Sudley Road, it formed, during the first battle, the anchor of the Confederate left and the objective of the Federal diversion under Tyler. Following the rout of McDowell's forces, it constituted one of the main avenues of escape. In the second battle, it was the main route of the Federal advance and retreat. Though the bridge was destroyed a number of times, the abutments are original. The present Lee Highway bridge crosses Bull Run about 100 feet south of the old structure which is now memorialized by the State of Virginia.

4. STONE HOUSE (MATTHEWS). Built in the early part of the nineteenth century, this two-and-one-half story structure of reddish brown native stone, stands as the best preserved and most conspicuous landmark on the two battlefields. It is located on the north side of Lee Highway, near its junction with the Manassas-Sudley Road. Here the tides of battle twice engulfed it as it served alternately as a hospital for the wounded of each side. Shells may still be seen embedded in its walls. For a number of years after the war it was operated as a tavern.

5. CHINN RIDGE. This commanding ridge was twice utilized by the Confederates in turning movements that brought defeat to Federal arms. In the first battle, the brigades of Early and Elzey, supported by Beckham's artillery, hurled back the Federal right under Howard to precipitate a general rout of the Federal army. In the second, Longstreet's troops swept forward to seize the ridge in an attack that, but for the successful defense of Henry Hill, would have turned the Federal left. The ridge is served by a park road which terminates at a commanding overlook at its northern end.

Site of the Chinn House. Only the foundation walls and the bases of two massive chimneys remain to attest what was once one of the most

The Stone House.

Looking east from Chinn Ridge to Henry Hill, showing the nature of the terrain that saw heavy fighting in both battles. The Henry House is shown on the left, the Visitor Center in center of photograph.

spacious residences on the Manassas battlefields. Built reputedly in the late eighteenth century, the house derived its name from Benjamin T. Chinn, who purchased the property in 1853. Twice used as a field hospital, it stood until 1950 when, in ruinous condition, it was dismantled.

Webster Monument. About 600 yards north of the Chinn House stands a granite boulder with bronze plaque marking the spot where Col. Fletcher Webster, son of the statesman, Daniel Webster, fell mortally wounded in the second battle, August 30, 1862. The boulder was brought from "Marshfield," Mass., the estate of the elder Webster.

Chinn Spring. Located on the north side of the Chinn House Road, a few yards from the little stream known as Chinn Branch, is Chinn Spring. Following the heat of battle, many of the exhausted and wounded soldiers of both armies came here to drink gratefully from its cool, bubbling waters. It is an attractive spot, shaded by tall oaks and marked by grass that is always green.

6. UNFINISHED RAILROAD. About 300 yards south of the present Sudley Church, the old grade of an independent line of the Manassas Gap Railroad crosses the Manasses-Sudley Road (State Route 234). Stretching southwestward from this point for a distance of nearly 2 miles is the section of the grade occupied by Jackson's troops during the

second battle. From this protecting screen he first revealed his position in the attack on King's column on August 28. Here, in the next 2 days, he successfully repelled repeated Federal assaults. Though brush and trees have grown up along much of it, the grade is still clearly defined.

7. SUDLEY CHURCH. Just west of the Manassas-Sudley Road, near its intersection with the Groveton-Sudley Road (State Route 622), stands Sudley Church on the approximate site of the wartime structure that twice served as a hospital. In the first battle, the Federal wounded overflowed the church into a number of neighboring houses.

8. "DEEP CUT." Approximately three-quarters of a mile northwest of Groveton and immediately in front of the old railroad grade is "Deep Cut," scene of the bitterest fighting of the second battle. Here the troops of Fitz-John Porter suffered terrific losses in gallant but vain attempts to penetrate Jackson's defenses. Heavy woods have now grown up in what was then open land largely obscuring the shaft of reddish brown stone erected to the memory of the Union troops who fell there. Most of the land of the "Deep Cut" area is not at present owned by the park.

9. THE DOGAN HOUSE. Here at Groveton, at the intersection of the Groveton-Sudley Road and Lee Highway, is located the Dogan House,

Wartime photograph of the Sudley Church. Courtesy Library of Congress.

The Dogan House.

one of the main landmarks of the second battle. It was across this area, on August 29, that Hood's division drove back the Union division of Hatch before it retired to the west of Groveton. The next day the area was involved in heavy artillery and infantry fire.

The small, one-story house of weather-boarded logs originally served as the overseer's house of the Dogan farm. Later, it was occupied by the Dogan family after their main house had burned. Like the Stone House, it now stands as one of the two remaining original structures in the park.

The Park

Manassas National Battlefield Park was designated a Federal area May 10, 1940. The more than 1,700 acres of Federal land in the park comprise parts of the two battlefields.

One of the initial steps in the memorialization of these fields was taken in 1922 with the purchase of the Henry Farm, of approximately 128 acres, by the Manassas Battlefield Confederate Park, Inc., and the Sons of Confederate Veterans. On March 19, 1938, the Henry Farm was conveyed by deed to the United States Government as an "everlasting memorial to the soldiers of the Blue and Gray." Significant additions to park holdings were made in 1949 with the acquisition of the historic Stone House and Dogan House properties.

How To Reach the Park

The park is situated in Prince William County, Va., 26 miles southwest of Washington, D. C. State Route 234 intersects U. S. 29 and 211 at the park boundary.

Administration

Manassas National Battlefield Park is administered by the National Park Service of the United States Department of the Interior. Communications should be addressed to the Superintendent, Manassas National Battlefield Park, Manassas, Va.

Related Areas

Other Civil War battlefields in Virginia administered by the National Park Service include: Fredericksburg and Spotsylvania National Military Park, Richmond National Battlefield Park, Petersburg National Military Park, and Appomattox Court House National Historical Park.

About Your Visit

A modern museum and battlefield markers are features of the park's interpretive program. The museum, which is highlighted by a diorama and an electric map, presents exhibits in such a way as to develop the story of both battles in narrative sequence. Free literature, library facilities, and interpretive services are also available at the museum. Special tours can be arranged for organizations and groups if advance notice is given to the superintendent. Museum hours are from 9 a. m. to 5 p. m. daily.

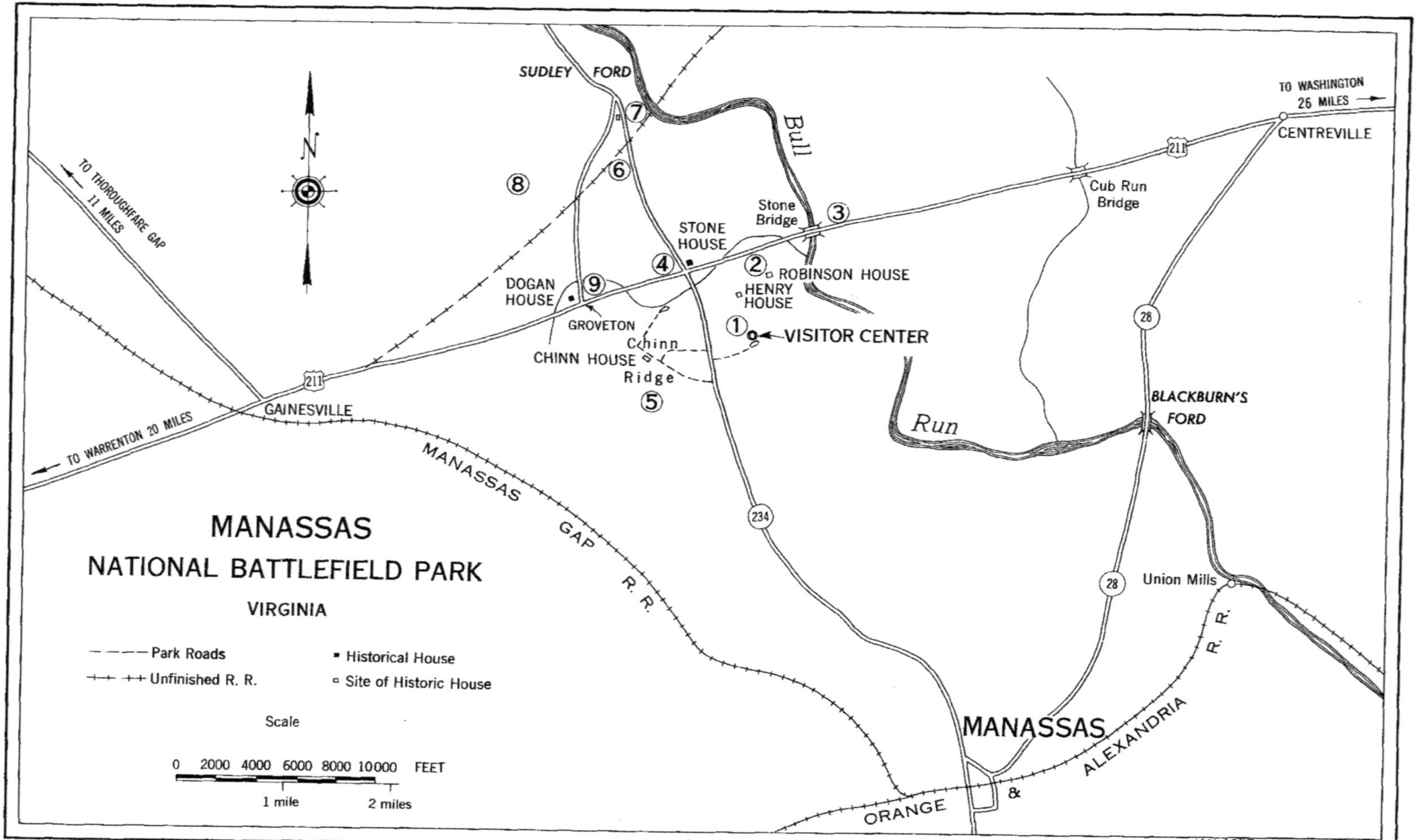

JAN. 1957 MNBP 7008

CPSIA information can be obtained
at www.ICGtesting.com
Printed in the USA
FFHW021804110419
51646965-57093FF

9 781582 187778